step-by-step
baking

step-by-step

baking

a visual step-by-step cookbook

This edition published by Parragon Books Ltd in 2015 and distributed by

Parragon Inc.
440 Park Avenue South, 13th Floor
New York, NY 10016
www.parragon.com/lovefood

LOVE FOOD is an imprint of Parragon Books Ltd

ISBN 978-1-4748-2439-2

Printed in China

Designed by Talking Design
Photography by Mike Cooper
Home economy by Lincoln Jefferson
New recipes by Christine France
Introduction by Linda Doeser

Notes for the Reader
This book uses metric, imperial, and US cup measurements. Follow the same units of measurements throughout; do not mix metric and imperial. All spoon and cup measurements are level unless otherwise indicated. Unless otherwise stated, milk is assumed to be whole, eggs are large, individual vegetables are medium, pepper is freshly ground black pepper, and salt is table salt. Unless otherwise stated, all root vegetables should be peeled prior to using.

The times given are an approximate guide only. Preparation times differ according to the techniques used by different people, and the cooking times may also vary from those given.

contents

introduction

This magnificent cookbook with its profusion of beautiful and immensely useful photographs will prove to be an invaluable addition to any cook's bookshelf. The recipes are clear, easy to follow, beautifully illustrated, and simply scrumptious, so whatever your level of expertise in the kitchen you are virtually guaranteed success every time.

Every recipe starts with a photograph of all the ingredients, but this is more than just a pretty picture or—even less helpful—a montage that is not to scale so that a pear appears to be the same size as an egg. Instead, it serves as a handy way of checking that you have everything ready before you start cooking. Just comparing the picture with the ingredients arranged on your own countertop or kitchen table will ensure that you haven't left anything out, and when it's time to add the candied cherries, for example, you have already quartered them as specified in the ingredients list. If you're uncertain about how thinly to slice fruit or how dark to toast nuts, a glance at the photograph will provide an instant answer.

Each short and straightforward step of the method is clearly explained without any jargon or difficult technical terms. Once again, what you see in the photograph is what you should expect to see in front of you. Not only is this reassuring for the novice cook, but those with more experience will find it a helpful reminder of the little touches that can easily be overlooked. Each recipe ends with a mouthwatering photograph of the finished cake, cookies, tart, or loaf.

Why you need this book

Even some experienced cooks will find "baking" a daunting prospect and think it's sure to be difficult. Yet the word baking encompasses many different kinds of products, from cookies to bread, and a variety of different techniques from creamed sponge cakes to choux pastry. They can't all be impossibly difficult and demanding and, in fact, most are astonishingly easy.

In this book there are 60 easy-to-follow recipes for cakes, traybakes, sweet and savory pastries, cookies, and bread—some traditional family favorites and others with a contemporary twist, some for special occasions and others for everyday treats. All of them are straightforward and, by using the unique frame-by-frame guide, even the novice cook will find they're figuratively and literally a piece of cake.

top tips for easy baking

> Read all the way through the recipe—ingredients list and method—before you start, so that you know exactly what you will need. Scrabbling about at the back of the pantry to find a rarely used ingredient or moving half a dozen other utensils to reach the one you need in the middle of preparing a cake batter or bread dough is, at best, exasperating and, at worst, liable to ruin it.

> Except when you are making pastry dough by the rubbing-in method, collect all your ingredients together, including anything that is normally stored in the refrigerator, at least half an hour before you start cooking to bring them to room temperature. Eggs are particularly important because if they are too cold when they are added, they tend to curdle. Remove mixing bowls from the cupboard to bring them to room temperature, too.

> When you are making pastry dough, collect the dry ingredients and any filling ingredients together ready for use and put a pitcher of water in the refrigerator to chill. (Keeping the dough cold is essential for crisp results.)

> Accurate measurement of the ingredients is more important for baking than for any other kind of cooking. Measure dry ingredients in standard kitchen cups and measure liquids in a measuring pitcher or, for small quantities, standard measuring spoons. Use medium eggs unless another size is specified in the recipe.

> Always preheat the oven to the specified temperature. An oven that is not hot enough will cause baked goods to sink, while one that is too hot can cause them to crack. If you're unsure about the reliability of your thermostat, invest in an oven thermometer and use that to check the temperature.

> The type of flour used for baking is important, and substituting one for another may produce disappointing results. All-purpose flour is used for pastry dough and anything that does not need a

a raising agent. Self-rising flour has added baking powder and is used for many different kinds of cakes. Bread flour has a high gluten content that produces an elastic dough when kneaded. Whole wheat flour is made from the whole grain and produces a denser, nuttier, slightly more chewy texture than white flour. If you do want to use it—in pastry dough, for example—substitute it with only half the quantity of white flour in the recipe. Whatever flour you are using, it is always worth sifting it to add air and remove any lumps, even if it is described as presifted on the package.

> Bread recipes often require yeast and may specify using lukewarm liquid. Yeast works best at a temperature of 70–97°F/21–36°C. Do not use hotter water because it will kill the yeast and prevent it from producing the gases that cause the bread to rise.

> Always use the size and shape of baking pan specified in the recipe. A pan that is too large will result in cracks and airholes and one that is too small is likely to cause the cake or loaf to burn.

> Follow the recipe instructions for cooling. Some cakes and cookies are fragile and should be left for a short while in the pan to become slightly firm before turning out onto a wire cooling rack. Others should be turned out onto the rack immediately after they have been removed from the oven or the bottom will become soggy. Heavy cakes are usually left in the pan to cool completely.

time-saving shortcuts

> Melt chocolate in the microwave oven. Break it into pieces and put it into a microwave-proof bowl. Heat on MEDIUM for 10 seconds, then stir. Return to the oven and heat for another 10 seconds before checking and stirring again—even when it's melted it will hold its shape, so you cannot tell if it's ready just by looking at it. White chocolate should be heated on LOW.

> Toast nuts in the microwave to avoid burning. Spread out 4 tablespoons of nuts on a microwave-proof plate and cook on HIGH for 5 minutes.

> All is not lost if you have forgotten to remove the butter from the refrigerator in advance—just microwave on HIGH for 15–20 seconds.

> The easiest way to peel fruit, such as nectarines and peaches, as well as tomatoes, is to slit their skins, put them into a heatproof bowl and pour in boiling water to cover. Let stand for 30–60 seconds and drain. The skins will slip off much more easily.

> When measuring small quantities of something sticky, such as honey or syrup, stand the spoon in hot water for a minute. It will then drop off the spoon easily.

> If dough is sticky, even after chilling in the refrigerator, roll it out between sheets of parchment paper or plastic wrap. You can use the bottom sheet to help you transfer it to the baking sheet.

useful equipment

> **Measuring cups:** It is important to be precise when measuring ingredients for baking. Always use standard kitchen measuring cups. These are available in sets, and some new ones even include cups in one-eighth measurements. If your set doesn't have these, 2 tablespoons equal one-eighth of a cup. When measuring dry ingredients, make sure they are level, using the back of a knife.

> **Measuring pitchers:** These are available in a variety of shapes and sizes. It is easier to measure liquids accurately using a tall, thin pitcher than a short fat one, and a clear pitcher is more useful than an opaque one.

> **Measuring spoons:** Ordinary spoons vary in size, so you will need at least one set of standard measuring spoons. As they are inexpensive, it's worth buying several sets to avoid having to keep washing them.

> **Mixing bowls:** You will need a selection of different sizes—large for mixing dough and cake batters, medium for measuring out ingredients, and small for melting chocolate, mixing frosting, and so on. Both heatproof glass and ceramic bowls are useful; metal bowls cannot be used in the microwave.

> **Sifters and strainers:** A sifter or strong fine wire strainer is essential for sifting dry ingredients to aerate them. A dredger or small strainer is useful for dusting cakes and cookies with confectioners' sugar.

> **Spoons and spatulas:** A set of wooden spoons in different sizes is invaluable for all kinds of tasks, from stirring a melted chocolate mixture in a hot pan to pressing fruit through a strainer. A long-handle metal spoon is perfect for folding dry ingredients into a whisked mixture. Flexible rubber or plastic spatulas, available in a variety of sizes, are useful for stirring, mixing, folding, and scraping all the cake batter out of the bowl.

> **Pastry blender:** This tool is used for working fat into flour rather than using your fingertips. It helps to keep the mixture cool but is not essential.

> **Whisks and blenders:** A handheld balloon whisk is useful for many tasks, from aerating egg whites to whisking cream. A handheld electric mixer takes the hard work out of these processes, is strong enough to cream butter and sugar mixtures, and can be used in a hot pan.

> **Rolling pin:** These can be made of wood, glass, marble, or plastic, and some can be filled with cold water to keep dough cool. Choose a heavy rolling pin that will do the job without your having to press down and so distort the dough.

> **Pastry board:** Marble is the best surface because it keeps the dough cool and requires only a very light dusting of flour. Wood is popular and, because it's a poor conductor of heat, it's also good for rolling out cookie doughs.

> **Cookie and pastry cutters:** These are available in a wide range of sizes and shapes with plain or fluted edges. Metal cutters produce a cleaner edge than plastic ones.

> **Cake pans:** Heavy-gauge cake pans distribute the heat evenly and prevent scorching. It is a matter of personal choice whether you prefer them with a nonstick lining. Round pans are used more often than other shapes, but always check the recipe. The most useful sizes are shallow 8-inch/20-cm round cake pans for sponge cakes and deep 9–10-inch/23–25-cm pans for larger cakes. A jelly roll pan is rectangular and shallow; you will need a slightly deeper rectangular pan for sheet cakes. Other special pans include springform pans, which have a clip on the side to make it easy to remove the pan from very fragile cakes, and angel cake pans, with a tube in the center projecting above the rim.

> **Loaf pans:** Bread is often baked on a flat baking sheet because the dough is dense enough to retain its shape. When a pan is used, the bottom and sides of the loaf are contained, so the dough expands upward, creating a denser crumb and crisp crust. Loaf pans are usually rectangular and popular sizes are 6½ x 4¼ x 3¼ inches/17 x 11 x 8 cm and 7½ x 4½ x 3½ inches/19 x 12 x 9 cm. They are available with nonstick linings.

> **Muffin and tart pans:** Available with a nonstick coating if you prefer, shallow muffin pans are perfect for small cakes and individual sweet or savory tarts. A 12-cup pan is a useful size. Muffin pans with deep cups have flared sides that encourage the dough to rise. Large tarts can be made in ovenproof glass or ceramic dishes, but metal ones distribute the heat more quickly and evenly. They are usually round and may be plain or fluted, with or without a removable bottom. They are available in a range of sizes. Deeper pans are best for tarts that require a firm crust to support a cream- or egg-based filling, while shallower pans are ideal for glazed fruit tarts.

> **Baking and cookie sheets:** It is best to buy heavy sheets because they do not buckle or wobble, and they distribute the heat evenly. Cookie sheets usually have a slightly sloping edge to make it easier to lift them and are used for many kinds of loaves, pastries, and cookies. Baking sheets have a rim around the entire edge to prevent runny mixtures from falling off.

> **Cooling rack:** Wire racks are made in a wide variety of shapes and sizes. They let air circulate around a cake or cookies, preventing trapped moisture from making them soggy while they cool.

cakes & traybakes

>4

>5

>6

classic cherry cake

serves 8

ingredients

generous ¾ cup unsalted
  butter, plus extra for greasing
1¼ cups candied cherries,
  quartered

scant 1 cup ground almonds
scant 1½ cups all-purpose flour
1 tsp baking powder
1 cup superfine sugar
3 large eggs

finely grated rind and juice
  of 1 lemon
6 sugar cubes, crushed

1 Preheat the oven to 350°F/180°C. Grease and line an 8-inch/20-cm round cake pan.

>2 Stir together the cherries, almonds, and 1 tablespoon of the flour. Sift the remaining flour into a separate bowl with the baking powder.

and sugar
ly add the
nly mixed.

>4 Add the flour mixture and fold lightly and evenly into the creamed mixture with a metal spoon. Add the cherry mixture, fold in evenly, then fold in the lemon rind and juice.

>5 Spoon the mixture into the prepared pan and sprinkle with the crushed sugar cubes. Bake in the preheated oven for 1–1¼ hours, or until risen and golden brown and shrinking from the sides of the pan.

>6 Let cool in the pan for 15 minutes, then turn out onto a wire rack to cool completely.

Cut into slices and serve.

chocolate fudge cake

serves 8

ingredients
¾ cup unsalted butter,
  softened, plus extra for
  greasing
generous ¾ cup superfine
  sugar

3 eggs, beaten
3 tbsp dark corn syrup
½ cup ground almonds
1¼ cup self-rising flour
pinch of salt
6 tbsp cocoa powder

frosting
8 oz/225 g semisweet dark
  chocolate, broken into pieces
¼ cup dark brown sugar
1 cup unsalted butter, diced

5 tbsp evaporated milk
½ tsp vanilla extract

> 1 Preheat the oven to 350°F/180°C. Grease and line two 8-inch/20-cm round cake pans.

> 2 For the frosting, place the ingredients in a heavy-bottomed saucepan. Heat gently, stirring constantly, until melted.

> 3 Pour into a bowl and let cool. Cover and chill for 1 hour, or until spreadable.

> 4 For the cake, place the butter and sugar in a bowl and beat together until light and fluffy. Gradually beat in the eggs. Stir in the corn syrup and almonds.

>5 Sift the flour, salt, and cocoa powder into a separate bowl, then fold into the mixture. Add a little water, if necessary, to make a dropping consistency.

>6 Spoon the mixture into the prepared cake pans and bake in the preheated oven for 30–35 minutes, or until springy to the touch and a skewer inserted in the center comes out clean.

>7 Cool in the pans for 5 minutes, then turn out onto a wire rack to cool completely.

>8 When the cakes are cold, sandwich them together with half the frosting. Spread the remaining frosting over the top and sides of the cake, swirling it to give a frosted appearance.

Cut into slices and serve.

sponge layer cake

serves 8

ingredients

¾ cup butter, softened,
  plus extra for greasing
1¼ cups self-rising flour
1 tsp baking powder
generous ¾ cup superfine
  sugar
3 eggs
confectioners' sugar, sifted, for
  dusting

filling

3 tbsp raspberry jam
1¼ cups heavy cream,
  whipped
16 fresh strawberries, halved

> **1** Preheat the oven to 350°F/180°C. Grease and line the bottom of two 8-inch/20-cm round cake pans.

> **2** Sift the flour and baking powder into a bowl and add the butter, sugar, and eggs. Mix together, then beat well until smooth. Divide the mixture evenly between the prepared pans and smooth the surfaces.

Dust with confectioners' sugar and serve.

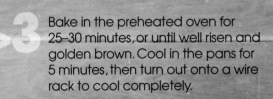

>3 Bake in the preheated oven for 25–30 minutes, or until well risen and golden brown. Cool in the pans for 5 minutes, then turn out onto a wire rack to cool completely.

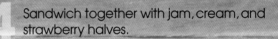

>4 Sandwich together with jam, cream, and strawberry halves.

banana coconut loaf cake

makes 1 loaf

ingredients

⅓ cup sunflower oil, plus extra
  for greasing
1¾ cups all-purpose flour
1½ tsp baking powder

1 cup superfine sugar
⅔ cup shredded coconut
2 eggs
2 ripe bananas, mashed
½ cup sour cream

1 tsp vanilla extract
shredded coconut, toasted,
  to decorate

1 Preheat the oven to 350°F/180°C. Grease and line an 8 × 4 × 2-inch/20 × 10 × 5-cm loaf pan.

 2 Sift together the flour and baking powder in a large bowl.

>3 Stir in the sugar and coconut.

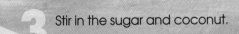

>4 Beat together the eggs, oil, bananas, cream, and vanilla extract in a large bowl.

5 Stir into the dry ingredients, mixing until evenly combined.

6 Spoon into the prepared pan, leveling with a palette knife.

7 Bake in the preheated oven for about 1 hour, or until risen, firm, and golden brown.

8 Cool in the pan for 15 minutes, then turn out onto a wire rack to cool completely.

Decorate with shreds of coconut and serve.

rich almond cake

serves 8

ingredients

butter, for greasing
generous 1 cup ricotta cheese
4 eggs, separated

1 tsp almond extract
generous ¾ cup sugar
2¾ cups ground almonds
finely grated rind of 1 lime

toasted slivered almonds,
  to decorate
confectioners' sugar, sifted,
  for dusting

>1 Preheat the oven to 300°F/150°C. Grease and line a 9-inch/23-cm round cake pan.

>2 Beat together the ricotta, egg yolks, almond extract, and sugar. Stir in the almonds and lime rind.

>3 Whisk the egg whites in a clean bowl until they form soft peaks.

>4 Fold the whites lightly into the ricotta mixture, using a large metal spoon.

33

>5 Spread the mixture in the pan and bake in the preheated oven for 50–60 minutes, until firm and lightly browned.

>6 Cool the cake in the pan for 10 minutes, then turn out onto a wire rack and sprinkle with slivered almonds. Leave to cool completely.

Dust with confectioners' sugar and serve.

double chocolate mint sponge

serves 8

ingredients
¾ cup unsalted butter,
  softened, plus extra for
  greasing
generous 1 cup all-purpose flour
2 tbsp cocoa powder
1 tbsp baking powder
generous ¾ cup superfine sugar
3 eggs, beaten
1 tbsp milk
1½ oz/40 g chocolate mint
  sticks, chopped
5 oz/140 g chocolate spread,
  plus extra to drizzle
chocolate mint sticks
  to decorate

> **>1** Preheat the oven to 350°F/180°C.
Grease and line two 8-inch/20-cm
round cake pans.

> **>2** Sift the flour, cocoa, and baking
powder into a bowl and beat in
the butter, sugar, and eggs, mixing
until smooth. Stir in the milk and
chocolate mint pieces.

Decorate the cake with chocolate mint sticks.

>3 Spread the mixture into the pans. Bake in the preheated oven for 25–30 minutes, until risen and firm. Cool in the pans for 2 minutes, then turn out onto a wire rack to cool completely.

>4 Sandwich the cakes together with chocolate spread. Gently warm a little of the spread and drizzle it over the top.

orange madeira ring

serves 8

ingredients

¾ cup unsalted butter, plus
  extra for greasing
1 tbsp dark corn syrup (plus
  extra for drizzling, if liked)

2 medium oranges
generous ¾ cup superfine sugar
3 eggs, beaten
generous ¾ cup all-purpose
  flour

generous ¾ cup self-rising flour
finely grated rind of 1 orange
2–3 tbsp orange juice

>1 Preheat the oven to 325°F/160°C. Grease a 1½-quart/1.5-liter ring cake pan and spoon the syrup into the bottom.

>2 Cut all the white peel and pith from the oranges and slice.

>3 Arrange the orange slices over the syrup in the pan.

>4 Cream together the butter and sugar until pale and fluffy.

5 Gradually beat in the eggs, beating well after each addition.

6 Sift the flours into the mixture and fold in, adding the orange rind and enough juice to make a soft consistency.

7 Spoon the mixture into the pan and smooth the surface.

8 Bake in the preheated oven for 45–55 minutes, or until risen, golden, and firm. Cool in the pan for 10 minutes, then turn out onto a wire rack to cool completely.

The cake can be served cold, or warm with extra dark corn syrup drizzled over.

caramel peach gâteau

serves 6–8

ingredients

¾ cup unsalted butter,
softened, plus extra for
greasing
generous ¾ cup light brown
sugar

3 eggs, beaten
1 tsp vanilla extract
1¼ cups self-rising flour
½ tsp baking powder
2 tbsp milk

filling

2 tbsp maple syrup
scant 1 cup thick crème
fraîche (40% fat)
3 ripe peaches, thinly sliced

>1 Preheat the oven to 350°F/180°C. Grease and line the bottom of two 9-inch/23-cm round cake pans.

>2 Place the butter, sugar, eggs, and vanilla extract in a bowl and sift over the flour and baking powder.

>3 Beat with an electric mixer until smooth, then add milk to make a soft consistency.

>4 Divide the mixture between the pans and spread evenly.

>5 Bake in the preheated oven for 25–30 minutes, until firm and golden. Cool in the pans for 2 minutes, then turn out onto a wire rack to cool completely.

>6 Swirl 1 tablespoon of maple syrup into the crème fraîche and spread half over each cake.

>7 Arrange half the peach slices over one cake and top with the remaining cake, crème fraîche side down.

>8 Arrange the remaining peach slices over the top of the cake.

Brush the peach slices with maple syrup just before serving. Serve the cake on the day of filling.

honey & almond cake

serves 12–16

ingredients
scant ¾ cup unsalted butter,
 plus extra for greasing
generous ½ cup light brown
 sugar
½ cup honey
1 tbsp lemon juice
2 eggs, beaten
scant 1½ cups self-rising flour
2 tbsp slivered almonds
warmed honey, to glaze

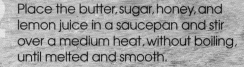

>1 Preheat the oven to 350°F/180°C. Grease and line a deep, 8-inch/ 20-cm cake pan.

>2 Place the butter, sugar, honey, and lemon juice in a saucepan and stir over a medium heat, without boiling, until melted and smooth.

Brush with the warmed honey
and cut into slices to serve.

>3 Remove the pan from the heat and
quickly beat in the eggs with a wooden
spoon. Sift in the flour and stir lightly with a
metal spoon. Pour into the prepared pan
and scatter the almonds over the top.

>4 Bake in the preheated oven for 35–40 minutes,
until risen, firm, and golden brown. Cool in the
pan for 15 minutes, then turn out onto a wire
rack to cool completely.

coffee & walnut roulade

serves 6

ingredients
butter or oil, for greasing
3 eggs
1 egg white
generous ½ cup superfine
   sugar, plus extra for sprinkling

1 tsp coffee extract
½ cup all-purpose flour, sifted
¼ cup finely chopped walnuts
roughly chopped walnuts,
   to decorate

filling
¾ cup heavy cream
⅓ cup confectioners' sugar,
   plus extra, sifted, for dusting
1 tbsp coffee liqueur

>1 Preheat the oven to 400°F/200°C. Grease a 13 x 8½-inch/33 x 22 cm-jelly roll pan and line with nonstick parchment paper.

>2 Place the eggs, egg white, and sugar in a bowl over a pan of very hot water. Whisk with an electric mixer until pale and thick enough to leave a trail.

>3 Whisk in the coffee extract, then fold in the flour and finely chopped walnuts lightly with a metal spoon.

>4 Spoon into the pan, spreading evenly. Bake in the preheated oven for 12–15 minutes, until golden brown and firm.

>5 Sprinkle a sheet of parchment paper with superfine sugar. Turn out the roulade onto the paper and peel off the lining paper. Trim the edges.

>6 Quickly roll up the sponge from one short side, with the paper inside. Cool completely.

>7 For the filling, place the cream, sugar, and liqueur in a bowl and whisk until the mixture begins to hold its shape.

>8 Carefully unroll the roulade, remove the paper and spread the cream over. Roll up carefully.

Serve the roulade dusted with confectioners' sugar and topped with roughly chopped walnuts.

blueberry & passionfruit drizzle squares

makes 9 squares

ingredients
scant ¾ cup butter, softened, plus extra for greasing
2 eggs

generous ¾ cup superfine sugar
1¼ cups self-rising flour, sifted
⅓ cup milk

finely grated zest of 1 lemon
1½ cups blueberries

syrup
4 ripe passionfruit
1 cup confectioners' sugar, plus extra, sifted, for dusting

>1 Preheat the oven to 375°F/190°C. Grease and line the bottom of a 9-inch/23-cm square cake pan.

>2 Whisk the butter, eggs, and sugar until pale and fluffy. Fold in the flour lightly and evenly.

>3 Stir in the milk, lemon zest, and 1¼ cups of the blueberries. Spread into the cake pan.

>4 Bake in the preheated oven for 25–30 minutes, until firm and golden brown. Remove from the oven and let cool in the pan.

>5 Meanwhile, make the syrup. Scoop the pulp from the passionfruit and rub through a strainer. Discard the pips.

>6 Place the confectioners' sugar and passionfruit juice in a saucepan and heat gently, stirring, until the sugar dissolves.

>7 Prick the warm cake with a fork, and spoon the syrup evenly over the surface.

>8 Let the cake cool completely in the pan, then cut into 9 squares.

Top the squares with the reserved blueberries and dust with confectioners' sugar before serving.

apple streusel bars

makes 14 bars

ingredients

generous ½ cup
  unsalted butter,
  softened, plus extra
  for greasing
2 crisp apples,
  peeled, cored,
  and diced
2 tbsp lemon juice
⅔ cup superfine
  sugar
1 tsp vanilla extract
2 eggs, beaten
generous 1 cup self-
  raising flour

topping

⅓ cup finely
  chopped,
  blanched almonds
¼ cup all-purpose
  flour
¼ cup light brown
  sugar
½ tsp ground
  cinnamon
2 tbsp unsalted
  butter, melted

> **1** Preheat the oven to 350°F/180°C. Grease and line an 11 x 7-inch/28 x 18-cm sheet cake pan. Sprinkle the apples with lemon juice.

> **2** Cream together the butter, sugar, and vanilla extract until pale. Gradually add the eggs, beating thoroughly.

Cut into bars and serve cold or warm.

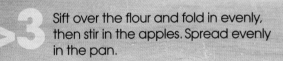
>3 Sift over the flour and fold in evenly, then stir in the apples. Spread evenly in the pan.

>4 For the topping, mix all the ingredients to a crumbly texture and sprinkle over the cake. Bake the cake in the preheated oven for 45–55 minutes, unti firm and golden.

frosted carrot cake

serves 16

ingredients

¾ cup sunflower oil,
  plus extra for greasing
generous ¾ cup light brown
  sugar
3 eggs, beaten

1½ cups grated carrots
½ cup golden raisins
⅓ cup walnut pieces
grated rind of 1 orange
1¼ cups self-rising flour
1 tsp baking soda

1 tsp ground cinnamon
½ tsp grated nutmeg
strips of orange zest,
  to decorate

frosting

scant 1 cup cream cheese
generous ¾ cup confectioners'
  sugar
2 tsp orange juice

> **1** Preheat the oven to 350°F/180°C. Grease and line a 9-inch/23-cm square cake pan.

> **2** In a large bowl, beat together the oil, sugar, and eggs. Stir in the grated carrots, raisins, walnut pieces, and orange rind.

> **3** Sift the flour, baking soda, cinnamon, and nutmeg together into the bowl, then mix evenly into the carrot mixture.

> **4** Spoon the mixture into the prepared cake pan. Bake in the preheated oven for 40–45 minutes, until well risen and firm to the touch.

5 Cool in the pan for 5 minutes, then turn out onto a wire rack to cool completely.

 6 For the frosting, mix the cheese, confectioners' sugar, and orange juice in a bowl and beat until smooth. Spread over the top of the cake and swirl with a palette knife.

Decorate with strips of orange zest and
serve cut into squares.

chocolate chip brownies

makes 12 brownies

ingredients

1 cup butter, softened, plus
  extra for greasing
5½ oz/150 g dark chocolate,
  broken into pieces

generous 1½ cups self-rising
  flour
²/₃ cup superfine sugar
4 eggs, beaten
½ cup chopped pistachio nuts

3½ oz/100 g white chocolate,
  roughly chopped
confectioners' sugar, sifted, for
  dusting

> **1** Preheat the oven to 350°F/180°C. Grease and line a 9-inch/23-cm square baking pan.

> **2** Place the dark chocolate and butter in a heatproof bowl set over a saucepan of simmering water. Stir until melted, then let cool slightly.

> **3** Sift the flour into a separate bowl and stir in the superfine sugar.

> **4** Stir the eggs into the chocolate mixture, then pour into the flour and sugar and beat well.

>5 Stir in the nuts and white chocolate.

>6 Pour the mixture into the prepared pan, using a palette knife to spread evenly.

>7 Bake in the preheated oven for 30–35 minutes, or until firm to the touch around the edges. Cool in the pan for 20 minutes, then turn out onto a wire rack to cool completely.

>8 Dust with confectioners' sugar and let cool completely.

Cut into 12 squares and serve.

cinnamon squares

makes 16 squares

ingredients

1 cup butter, softened,
  plus extra for greasing
generous 1 cup superfine
  sugar
3 eggs, lightly beaten
1²/₃ cups self-rising
  flour
½ tsp baking soda
1 tbsp ground cinnamon
²/₃ cup sour cream
¹/₃ cup sunflower
  seeds

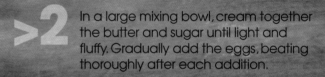

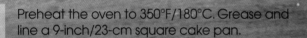

>**1** Preheat the oven to 350°F/180°C. Grease and
line a 9-inch/23-cm square cake pan.

>**2** In a large mixing bowl, cream together
the butter and sugar until light and
fluffy. Gradually add the eggs, beating
thoroughly after each addition.

Cut into 16 squares and serve.

>3 Sift the flour, baking soda, and cinnamon into the creamed mixture and fold in with a metal spoon. Mix in the sour cream and sunflower seeds until well combined. Spoon into the prepared pan and smooth the surface with the back of a spoon.

>4 Bake in the preheated oven for about 45 minutes, until firm to the touch. Loosen the edges and turn out onto a wire rack to cool completely.

pastries

>4

>5

>6

cinnamon swirls

makes 12 swirls

ingredients

2 tbsp butter, cut into small
  pieces, plus extra for greasing
generous 1½ cups white
  bread flour

½ tsp salt
1 envelope active dry yeast
1 egg, lightly beaten
½ cup lukewarm milk
2 tbsp maple syrup, for glazing

filling

4 tbsp butter, softened
2 tsp ground cinnamon
¼ cup light brown sugar
⅓ cup currants

 **>1** Grease a baking sheet and a bowl. Sift the flour and salt into a mixing bowl and stir in the yeast.

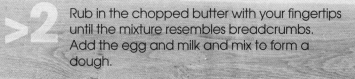 **>2** Rub in the chopped butter with your fingertips until the mixture resembles breadcrumbs. Add the egg and milk and mix to form a dough.

>3 Form the dough into a ball, place in the greased bowl, cover, and let stand in a warm place for about 40 minutes, or until doubled in volume.

>4 Punch down the dough lightly for 1 minute, then roll out to a rectangle measuring 12 x 19 inches/30 x 23 cm.

>5 For the filling, cream together the softened butter, cinnamon, and sugar until light and fluffy.

>6 Spread the filling over the dough, leaving a 1-inch/2.5-cm border. Sprinkle the currants evenly over the top. Roll up the dough from one of the long edges and press down to seal.

>7 Preheat the oven to 375°F/190°C. Cut the roll into 12 slices and place them, cut side down, on the prepared baking sheet. Cover and let stand for 30 minutes.

>8 Bake in the preheated oven for 20–30 minutes, or until the swirls are well risen.

Brush with maple syrup and let cool slightly before serving.

strawberry éclairs

makes 16–18 éclairs

ingredients

pastry
4 tbsp unsalted butter,
  plus extra for greasing
²/₃ cup water
½ cup all-purpose flour, sifted
2 eggs, beaten

filling
7 oz/200 g strawberries
2 tbsp confectioners' sugar
5 oz/140 g mascarpone cheese

>1 Preheat the oven to 425°F/220°C. Grease 2 baking sheets. Heat the butter and water in a pan until boiling.

>2 Remove from the heat, quickly tip in the flour, and beat until smooth. Transfer to a bowl.

>3 Gradually beat in the eggs with an electric handheld mixer, until glossy.

>4 Spoon into a piping bag with a large plain nozzle and pipe up to eighteen 3½-inch/9-cm fingers on the baking sheets.

>5 Bake in the preheated oven for 12–15 minutes, until golden brown. Cut a slit down the side of each éclair to release steam. Bake for another 2 minutes. Cool on a wire rack.

>6 Puree half the strawberries with the confectioners' sugar.

>7 Finely chop the remaining strawberries and stir into the mascarpone.

>8 Pipe or spoon the mascarpone mixture into the éclairs.

Serve the éclairs with the strawberry puree spooned over. The éclairs are best served within an hour of filling.

chocolate filo parcels

makes 18 parcels

ingredients
4–6 tbsp butter, melted, plus
  extra for greasing
1 cup ground hazelnuts
1 tbsp finely chopped fresh
  mint
½ cup sour cream
2 apples, peeled and grated
2 oz/55 g semisweet dark
  chocolate, melted
9 sheets filo pastry, about
  6 inches/15 cm square
confectioners' sugar, sifted, for
  dusting

> **1** Preheat the oven to 375°F/190°C. Grease
a baking sheet. Mix the nuts, mint, and sour
cream in a bowl. Add the apples, stir in the
chocolate, and mix well.

> **2** Cut each pastry sheet into 4 squares.
Brush 1 square with butter, then
place a second square on top and
brush with butter.

Dust with confectioners' sugar and serve.

>3 Place a tablespoonful of the chocolate mixture in the center, bring up the corners, and twist together. Repeat until all of the pastry and filling has been used.

>4 Place the parcels on the prepared baking sheet and bake in the preheated oven for about 10 minutes, until crisp and golden. Remove from the oven and let cool slightly.

79

apple danish
makes 12–16 pastries

ingredients
2 cups white bread flour, plus
  extra, sifted, for dusting
¾ cup butter, well chilled, plus
  extra for greasing

½ tsp salt
1 envelope active dry yeast
2 tbsp superfine sugar, plus
  extra for sprinkling
1 egg

1 tsp vanilla extract
6 tbsp lukewarm water
milk, for glazing

filling
2 cooking apples, peeled,
  cored, and chopped
grated rind of 1 lemon
3 tbsp sugar

>1 Place the flour in a bowl, rub in 2 tablespoons of the butter, and set aside. Dust the remaining butter with flour, grate coarsely into a bowl, and chill. Stir the salt, yeast, and sugar into the flour mixture.

>2 In another bowl, beat the egg with the vanilla extract and water, add to the flour mixture, and mix to form a dough. Knead for 10 minutes on a floured surface, then chill for 10 minutes.

>3 Roll out the dough to a 12 x 8-inch/30 x 20-cm rectangle. Mark widthwise into thirds and fold. Press the edges with a rolling pin and roll out to the same size as the original rectangle.

>4 Sprinkle the grated butter evenly over the top two-thirds. Fold up the bottom third and fold down the top third. Press the edges, wrap in plastic wrap, and chill for 30 minutes. Repeat four times, chilling each time. Chill overnight.

> **5** Mix together the filling ingredients. Preheat the oven to 400°F/ 200°C. Grease two baking sheets.

> **6** Roll out the dough into a 16-inch/40-cm square and cut up to 16 squares. Pile some filling in the center of each, reserving any juice. Brush the edges of the squares with milk and bring the corners together in the center.

> **7** Place on the prepared baking sheets and chill for 15 minutes. Brush with the reserved juice and sprinkle with superfine sugar.

> **8** Bake in the preheated oven for 10 minutes, reduce the temperature to 350°F/180°C, and bake for another 10–15 minutes, until browned.

Gently remove from the baking sheets and serve.

date, pistachio nut & honey slices

makes 12 slices

ingredients

scant 1½ cups chopped,
  pitted dates
2 tbsp lemon juice
2 tbsp water

⅔ cup chopped pistachio nuts
2 tbsp honey
milk, for glazing

pastry

scant 1⅔ cups all-purpose
  flour, sifted
2 tbsp superfine sugar
scant ¾ cup butter
4–5 tbsp cold water, to mix

>1 Place the dates, lemon juice, and water in a pan and bring to a boil, stirring. Remove from the heat.

>2 Stir in the pistachio nuts and 1 tablespoon of honey, cover, and let cool.

>3 Preheat the oven to 400°F/200°C. For the pastry, place the flour, sugar, and butter in a food processor and process until the mixture resembles fine breadcrumbs.

>4 Mix in just enough cold water to bind to a soft, not sticky, dough.

>5 Roll out the pastry on a floured surface to two 12 x 8-inch/30 x 20-cm rectangles. Place one on a baking sheet.

>6 Spread the date-and-nut mixture to within ½ inch/1 cm of the edge. Top with the remaining pastry.

>7 Press to seal, trim the edges, and mark into 12 slices. Glaze with milk.

>8 Bake in the preheated oven for 20–25 minutes, until golden. Brush with the remaining honey and cool on a wire rack.

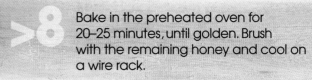

Cut into slices and serve as a
lunch-bag snack.

chocolate nut strudel

serves 6

ingredients
scant ¾ cup unsalted
 butter, melted, plus extra
 for greasing
7 oz/200 g mixed
 chopped nuts
4 oz/115 g dark
 chocolate, chopped
4 oz/115 g milk
 chocolate, chopped
4 oz/115 g white
 chocolate, chopped
7 oz/200 g filo pastry
3 tbsp dark corn syrup
½ cup confectioners' sugar,
 sifted, for dusting

>**1** Preheat the oven to 375°F/190°C. Lightly
grease a baking sheet. Reserving a
tablespoonful, place the nuts in a bowl
and mix with the chocolate.

>**2** Place a sheet of pastry on a clean
dish towel. Brush with butter, drizzle
with corn syrup, and sprinkle with the
nut-and-chocolate mixture. Place
another sheet on top and repeat the
procedure until you have used all
the nuts and chocolate.

Dust the strudel with confectioners' sugar, slice, and serve.

>3 Use the dish towel to carefully roll up the strudel, place on the prepared baking sheet, drizzle with the remaining corn syrup, and sprinkle with the reserved nuts.

>4 Bake in the preheated oven for 20–25 minutes. If the nuts start to brown too much, cover the strudel with a sheet of foil.

89

spiced pear & golden raisin strudel

serves 6

ingredients

6 tbsp unsalted butter, melted, plus extra for greasing
3 firm ripe pears, peeled, cored, and diced

finely grated rind and juice of ½ lemon
⅓ cup raw brown sugar
1 tsp ground allspice
⅓ cup golden raisins

⅔ cup ground almonds
6 sheets filo pastry (half a 9 oz/250 g package)
confectioners' sugar, sifted, for dusting

>1 Preheat the oven to 400°F/200°C and grease a baking sheet with butter.

>2 Mix together the pears, lemon rind and juice, sugar, allspice, raisins, and half the almonds.

>3 Place 2 sheets of filo pastry, slightly overlapping, on a clean dish towel.

>4 Brush lightly with melted butter and sprinkle with one-third of the almonds. Top with two more sheets, butter, and almonds. Repeat once more.

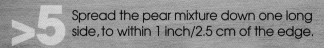

>5 Spread the pear mixture down one long side, to within 1 inch/2.5 cm of the edge.

>6 Roll the pastry over to enclose the filling and roll up, using the dish towel to lift. Tuck the ends under.

>7 Brush with a little melted butter and bake in the preheated oven for 20–25 minutes, until golden and crisp.

>8 Lightly dust the strudel with confectioners' sugar.

Serve the strudel warm or cold, cut into
thick slices.

baklava

serves 16

ingredients

2¼ cups walnut halves, finely
   chopped
1¾ cups shelled pistachio nuts,
   finely chopped
¾ cup blanched almonds,
   finely chopped

4 tbsp pine nuts, finely
   chopped
finely grated rind of 2 large
   oranges
6 tbsp sesame seeds
1 tbsp sugar
½ tsp ground cinnamon

½ tsp allspice
generous 1 cup butter, melted,
   plus extra for greasing
23 sheets filo pastry

syrup
1¼ cups superfine sugar

2 cups water
5 tbsp honey
3 cloves

> **1** Put the walnuts, pistachios, almonds, and pine nuts in a bowl and stir in the orange rind, sesame seeds, sugar, cinnamon, and allspice.

> **2** Preheat the oven to 325°F/160°C. Grease a 10-inch/25-cm square ovenproof dish, about 2 inches/5 cm deep.

> **3** Stack the pastry sheets. Cut them to the size of the dish, using a ruler.

> **4** Place a sheet of pastry on the bottom of the dish and brush with melted butter. Top with seven more sheets, brushing with butter between each layer.

> 5 Sprinkle with one-fifth of the filling. Top with three sheets of pastry, brushing each one with butter. Continue until you have used all the pastry and filling, ending with a top layer of three sheets.

> 6 Brush with butter. Cut into 2-inch/5-cm squares. Brush again with butter. Bake in the preheated oven for 1 hour.

> 7 Meanwhile, put all the syrup ingredients in a saucepan. Slowly bring to a boil, stirring to dissolve the sugar, then simmer for 15 minutes, without stirring, until a thin syrup forms. Let cool.

> 8 Remove the baklava from the oven and strain the syrup over the top. Let cool in the dish.

Cut into squares and serve.

fruit-filled tartlets

makes 12 tartlets

ingredients
scant 1½ cups all-purpose
  flour, plus extra for dusting
¾ cup confectioners' sugar,
  sifted
²/₃ cup ground almonds
½ cup butter
1 egg yolk
1 tbsp milk

filling
1 cup cream cheese
confectioners' sugar, to taste,
  plus extra, sifted, for dusting
12 oz/350 g fresh berries, such
  as raspberries, strawberries,
  and blueberries

> **1** Sift the flour and confectioners' sugar into
a bowl. Stir in the almonds. Add the butter,
rubbing in until the mixture resembles
breadcrumbs. Add the egg yolk and milk
and work in until the dough binds together.
Wrap in plastic wrap and chill for 30 minutes.

> **2** Preheat the oven to 400°F/200°C. Roll
out the dough on a lightly floured
surface and use it to line 12 deep
tartlet pans. Prick the bottoms and
press a piece of foil into each.

Dust with sifted confectioners'
sugar and serve immediately.

>3 Bake in the preheated oven for
10–15 minutes, or until light golden
brown. Remove the foil and bake for
another 2–3 minutes. Transfer to a wire
rack to cool.

>4 Halve the strawberries. For the filling, mix
together the cream cheese and confectioners'
sugar in a bowl. Place a spoonful of filling in
each tartlet and arrange the berries on top.

apple pie

serves 6–8

ingredients

1¼ cups all-purpose flour
pinch of salt
6 tbsp butter, cut into pieces

scant ½ cup lard, cut into small
   pieces
about 1–2 tbsp cold water
beaten egg or milk, for glazing

filling

1 lb 10 oz–2 lb 4 oz/750 g–1 kg
   cooking apples, peeled,
   cored, and sliced

²/₃ cup light brown sugar, plus
   extra for sprinkling
½–1 tsp ground cinnamon
about 1–2 tbsp water

>1 Sift the flour and salt into a mixing bowl. Add the butter and lard, and rub in with your fingertips until the mixture resembles fine breadcrumbs.

>2 Add enough water to mix to a firm dough. Wrap in plastic wrap and chill for 30 minutes.

>3 Preheat the oven to 425°F/220°C. Thinly roll out almost two-thirds of the pastry and use to line a deep 9-inch/23-cm pie plate.

>4 For the filling, mix the apples with the sugar and cinnamon, and pack into the pastry shell.

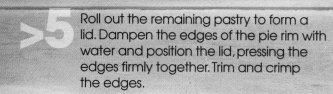 **>5** Roll out the remaining pastry to form a lid. Dampen the edges of the pie rim with water and position the lid, pressing the edges firmly together. Trim and crimp the edges.

 >6 Use the pastry trimmings to cut out leaves or other shapes. Dampen and attach to the top of the pie.

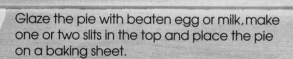 **>7** Glaze the pie with beaten egg or milk, make one or two slits in the top and place the pie on a baking sheet.

 >8 Bake in the preheated oven for 20 minutes, then reduce the temperature to 350°F/180°C and bake for another 30 minutes, or until the pastry is a light golden brown.

Sprinkle with sugar and serve hot or cold.

lemon meringue pie

serves 6–8

ingredients

generous 1 cup all-purpose
 flour, plus extra for dusting
6 tbsp butter, cut into small
 pieces, plus extra for greasing

⅓ cup confectioners' sugar,
 sifted
finely grated rind of ½ lemon
½ egg yolk, beaten
1½ tbsp milk

filling

3 tbsp cornstarch
1¼ cups water
juice and grated rind of
 2 lemons

generous ¾ cup superfine
 sugar
2 eggs, separated

>**1** Sift the flour into a bowl. Rub in the butter with your fingertips until the mixture looks like fine breadcrumbs. Mix in the confectioners' sugar, lemon rind, egg yolk, and milk.

>**2** Knead briefly on a lightly floured work surface. Wrap in plastic wrap and chill in the refrigerator for 30 minutes.

>**3** Preheat the oven to 350°F/180°C. Grease an 8-inch/20-cm round tart pan. Roll out the pastry to ¼ inch/5 mm thick, then use it to line the pan.

>**4** Prick all over with a fork, line with parchment paper, and fill with dried beans. Bake in the preheated oven for 15 minutes.

>5 Remove the pastry shell from the oven and take out the paper and beans. Reduce the temperature to 300°F/150°C.

>6 For the filling, mix the cornstarch with a little water to form a paste. Put the remaining water in a saucepan. Stir the lemon juice and rind into the cornstarch paste. Bring to a boil, stirring. Cook for 2 minutes. Cool slightly.

>7 Stir in 5 tablespoons of the superfine sugar and the egg yolks, and pour the mixture into the pastry shell.

>8 Whisk the egg whites in a clean, grease-free bowl until stiff. Gradually whisk in the remaining superfine sugar and spread over the pie. Place on a baking sheet and bake for 40 minutes. Remove from the oven and cool.

Serve plain or decorate with whipped cream and fresh fruit.

cherry & cinnamon tartlets

makes 4 tartlets

ingredients

generous ¾ cup all-purpose
  flour, sifted
2 tbsp confectioners' sugar,
  sifted
½ tsp ground cinnamon
5 tbsp unsalted butter, softened
1 egg yolk
2 tbsp cold water

filling

12 oz/350 g cherries, pitted
²/₃ cup Greek-style yogurt, or
  strained plain yogurt
2 tbsp honey
cinnamon and whole cherries,
  to decorate

>1 Preheat the oven to 375°F/190°C. Place the flour, sugar, cinnamon, and butter in a food processor and process until evenly blended.

>2 Add the egg yolk and water to the mixture, and blend until it just binds to form a soft dough.

Drizzle the tartlets with honey, sprinkle with cinnamon, and serve with whole cherries.

> 3 Divide the pastry into four and press into four 4-inch/18-cm/loose-bottom tartlet pans, pressing with your knuckles to spread evenly.

> 4 Place on a baking sheet, prick the bottoms with a fork, and bake the tartlets lined with foil for 12–15 minutes (see page 98), then remove from the oven and let cool. Stir the cherries into the yogurt and spoon into the shells.

109

broccoli, pancetta & bleu cheese galette

serves 4

ingredients
1 sheet puff pastry (half a
  package)
generous 3 cups small broccoli
  florets, halved if necessary
4½ oz/125 g diced pancetta

1 small red onion, sliced
3½ oz/100 g bleu cheese,
  chopped
ground black pepper
toasted pine nuts, to garnish

>1 Preheat the oven to 400°F/200°C. Place the pastry on a baking sheet and lightly score a line all around, cutting only halfway through, to within ½ inch/1 cm of the edge.

>2 Steam or boil the broccoli for 4–5 minutes, until just tender. Drain.

>3 Fry the pancetta with the onion, stirring, until golden. Stir in the broccoli and season with black pepper.

>4 Spread the filling over the pastry, leaving the border clear.

5 Scatter the pieces of cheese evenly over the top.

6 Bake in the preheated oven for 25–30 minutes, until the pastry is risen and golden.

Sprinkle with toasted pine nuts and
serve warm.

upside-down tomato tart

serves 4

ingredients
2 tbsp butter
1 tbsp superfine sugar
1 lb 2 oz/500 g cherry
  tomatoes, halved
1 clove garlic, crushed

2 tsp white wine vinegar
salt and pepper

pastry
1¾ cups all-purpose flour, sifted
pinch of salt

generous ½ cup butter
1 tbsp chopped oregano,
  plus extra to garnish
5-6 tbsp cold water

> **1** Preheat the oven to 400°F/200°C. Melt the butter in a heavy-bottom pan.

> **2** Add the sugar and stir over a high heat until just turning golden brown.

> **3** Remove from the heat and quickly add the tomatoes, garlic, and white wine vinegar, stirring to coat evenly. Season with salt and pepper.

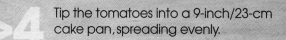

> **4** Tip the tomatoes into a 9-inch/23-cm cake pan, spreading evenly.

>5 For the pastry, place the flour, salt, butter, and oregano in a food processor and process until the mixture resembles fine breadcrumbs.

>6 Add just enough water to bind to a soft, but not sticky, dough.

>7 Roll out the pastry to a 10-inch/25-cm circle and place over the tomatoes, tucking in the edges. Pierce with a fork to let out steam.

>8 Bake in the preheated oven for 25–30 minutes, until firm and golden. Rest for 2–3 minutes, then run a knife around the edge and turn out onto a warmed serving plate.

Sprinkle the tart with chopped oregano
and serve warm.

asparagus prosciutto wraps

makes 6 wraps

ingredients

8 oz/225 asparagus,
  trimmed
13 oz/375 g chilled puff
  pastry sheet
2 tbsp pesto
6 thin slices prosciutto
¾ cup grated Emmental
  cheese
milk, for glazing
ground black pepper

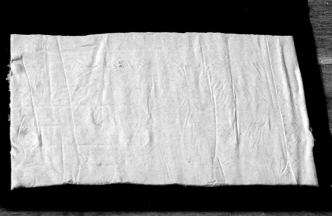

> **1** Preheat the oven to 425°F/220°C. Cook the asparagus in boiling water for 5–6 minutes, until tender. Drain.

> **2** Cut the pastry into 6 squares. Place on a baking sheet and spread 1 teaspoon of pesto on the center of each.

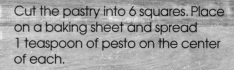

Serve the wraps warm or cold, as a lunchtime snack or picnic treat.

>3 Divide the asparagus into six bunches and wrap each in a prosciutto slice. Place diagonally on each square and top with grated cheese and pepper.

>4 Lift opposite corners over to meet on top, brushing with milk to glaze. Bake in the preheated oven for 15–20 minutes, until golden.

>1

>2

>3

small cakes
& cookies

>4

>5

>6

frosted peanut butter cupcakes

makes 16 cupcakes

ingredients
4 tbsp butter, softened
generous 1 cup light brown
 sugar
½ cup crunchy peanut butter
2 eggs, lightly beaten

1 tsp vanilla extract
generous 1½ cups all-purpose
 flour
2 tsp baking powder
scant ½ cup milk

frosting
scant 1 cup cream cheese
2 tbsp butter, softened
2 cups confectioners' sugar

> **1** Preheat the oven to 350°F/180°C. Put 16 double-layer paper liners on a baking sheet.

> **2** Put the butter, sugar, and peanut butter in a bowl and beat together until well mixed. Gradually add the eggs, beating well after each addition, then add the vanilla extract.

> **3** Sift in the flour and baking powder into a bowl, then use a metal spoon to fold in, alternating with the milk.

> **4** Spoon the mixture into the paper liners and bake in the preheated oven for 25 minutes, or until well risen and golden brown. Transfer to a wire rack and let cool.

>**5** For the frosting, put the cream cheese and butter into a large bowl and beat together until smooth. Sift in the confectioners' sugar, then beat until well mixed.

>**6** When the cupcakes are cold, spread some frosting on top of each, swirling with a round-bladed knife.

Store in the refrigerator until ready to serve.

chocolate butterfly cupcakes

makes 12 cupcakes

ingredients
generous ¾ cup soft margarine
⅔ cup superfine sugar
generous 1 cup self-rising flour,
  sifted
2 large eggs
2 tbsp cocoa powder
1 oz/ 25 g semisweet dark
  chocolate, melted

lemon buttercream
7 tbsp unsalted butter, softened
2 cups confectioners' sugar,
  sifted, plus extra for dusting
grated rind of ½ lemon
1 tbsp lemon juice

>1 Preheat the oven to 350°F/180°C. Place 12 paper liners in a shallow muffin pan.

>2 Place the margarine, superfine sugar, flour, eggs, and cocoa powder in a large bowl, and beat until the mixture is just smooth. Beat in the melted chocolate.

>3 Spoon the mixture into the paper liners, filling them three-quarters full.

>4 Bake in the preheated oven for 15 minutes, or until well risen. Transfer to a wire rack and let cool completely.

>5 For the buttercream, place the butter in a mixing bowl and beat until fluffy. Gradually add in the confectioners' sugar, lemon rind, and lemon juice, beating well with each addition.

>6 Cut the top off each cake, using a serrated knife. Cut each cake top in half. Spread the lemon buttercream over the cut surface of each cake and push the two pieces of cake top into the frosting to form wings.

Dust with confectioners' sugar.

classic cupcakes

makes 16 cupcakes

ingredients

½ cup unsalted butter
generous ½ cup superfine
 sugar
2 eggs, beaten
¾ cup self-rising flour
sugar flowers, colored
 sprinkles, candied cherries,
 and/or chocolate strands, to
 decorate

icing

1¾ cups confectioners' sugar
about 2 tbsp lukewarm water
few drops of food coloring
 (optional)

>1 Preheat the oven to 350°F/180°C. Put 16
double-layer paper liners on a baking sheet.

>2 Place the butter and superfine sugar
in a large bowl and cream together
until pale and fluffy. Gradually add
the eggs, beating well after each
addition. Fold in the flour, using a
metal spoon.

Decorate the cupcakes with sugar flowers, colored sprinkless, and candied cherries, and serve.

>3 Spoon the mixture into the paper liners and bake in the preheated oven for 15–20 minutes, until well risen. Remove from the oven and place on a wire rack to cool.

>4 For the icing, sift the confectioners' sugar into a bowl and add enough water to mix to a smooth paste, thick enough to coat the back of a spoon. Stir in a few drops of food coloring, if using, then spread over the cakes.

double ginger cupcakes

makes about 12 cupcakes

ingredients

1¼ cups all-purpose flour
1 tbsp baking powder
2 tsp ground ginger
¾ cup unsalted butter,
  softened

generous ¾ cup light brown
  sugar
3 eggs, beaten
1 oz/25 g preserved ginger,
  finely chopped

frosting

scant 1 cup ricotta cheese
¾ cup confectioners' sugar,
  sifted
finely grated rind 1 tangerine

diced preserved ginger,
  to decorate

>1 Preheat the oven to 375°F/190°C. Place 12 paper liners in shallow muffin pans.

>2 Sift the flour, baking powder, and ground ginger into a large bowl.

>3 Add the butter, brown sugar, and eggs and beat well until smooth. Stir in the preserved ginger.

>4 Spoon the mixture into the paper liners. Bake in the preheated oven for 15–20 minutes, until well risen. Cool on a wire rack.

> **5** For the frosting, mix together the ricotta, confectioners' sugar, and tangerine rind until smooth.

> **6** Spoon a little frosting onto each cake and spread over the surface to cover.

Top the cupcakes with diced preserved ginger and serve.

lowfat blueberry muffins

makes 12 muffins

ingredients

scant 1²/₃ cups all-purpose flour
1 tsp baking soda
¼ tsp salt

1 tsp ground allspice
generous ½ cup superfine
  sugar
3 large egg whites

3 tbsp lowfat margarine
²/₃ cup thick lowfat plain
  yogurt or blueberry-flavored
  yogurt

1 tsp vanilla extract
3 oz 85 g/fresh blueberries

>1 Preheat the oven to 375°F/190°C. Place 12 paper liners in a shallow muffin pan.

>2 Sift the flour, baking soda, salt, and half the allspice into a large mixing bowl. Add half the sugar and mix together well.

>3 In a separate bowl, whisk the egg whites together. Add the margarine, yogurt, and vanilla extract and mix together well, then stir in the blueberries until thoroughly mixed.

>4 Add the fruit mixture to the dry ingredients, then gently stir until just combined. Do not overstir—it is fine for it to be a little lumpy.

>5 Divide the mixture evenly between the paper liners to about two-thirds full. Mix the remaining sugar with the remaining allspice and sprinkle over the muffins.

>6 Bake in the preheated oven for 25 minutes, or until well risen. Remove the muffins from the oven.

Let cool or serve warm.

lemon poppy seed madeleines

makes about 30 madeleines

ingredients
oil, for greasing
3 eggs
1 egg yolk
finely grated rind of
 1 lemon
¾ cup superfine sugar
1 cup all-purpose flour
1 tsp baking powder
generous ½ cup unsalted
 butter, melted and
 cooled
1 tbsp poppy seeds

> **1** Preheat the oven to 375°F/190°C. Lightly grease three 12-hole madeleine pans.

> **2** Whisk the eggs, yolk, lemon rind, and sugar in a large bowl until very pale and thick.

Turn out the cakes and cool
on a wire rack, then serve
very fresh.

>3 Sift the flour and baking powder over the
mixture and fold in lightly using a metal
spoon. Fold in the melted butter and
poppy seeds.

>4 Spoon into the pans and bake in the
preheated oven for about 10 minutes,
until well risen.

apricot, macadamia & white chocolate chunk muffins

makes 12 muffins

ingredients

2 cups all-purpose flour
1 tbsp baking powder
generous ½ cup superfine
  sugar
½ cup chopped, plumped,
  dried apricots
⅓ cup chopped macadamia
  nuts
2 oz/55 g white chocolate,
  chopped
2 eggs, beaten
scant 1 cup buttermilk
scant ½ cup sunflower oil

>1 Preheat the oven to 400°F/200°C. Place 12 paper muffin liners in a muffin pan or on a baking sheet.

>2 Sift the flour and baking powder into a bowl and stir in the sugar, apricots, nuts, and chocolate.

Serve the muffins warm, preferably on the day of making.

> **>3** Beat together the eggs, buttermilk, and oil, then add to the bowl and stir to mix evenly.

> **>4** Spoon the mixture into the muffin liners and bake in the preheated oven for 20–25 minutes, until well risen.

cornmeal berry crunch cakes

makes 18 cakes

ingredients

1²/₃ cups self-rising flour, sifted
²/₃ cup cornmeal
¾ cup superfine sugar
scant ¾ cup unsalted butter
finely grated rind of 1 lemon

1 egg, beaten
2–3 tbsp lemon juice
5½ oz/150 g mixed berries

>1 Preheat the oven to 400°F/200°C. Place 18 paper liners in two shallow muffin pans.

>2 Place the flour, cornmeal, sugar, and butter in a food processor and process to resemble fine breadcrumbs.

>3 Stir the lemon rind into the mixture.

>4 Stir in the egg with just enough lemon juice to make a soft, crumbly dough.

>5 Fold in the berries with a metal spoon, mixing evenly.

>6 Spoon the mixture into the cake liners and bake for about 20 minutes, until golden brown. Cool the cakes on a wire rack.

The cakes can be stored for
2–3 days in an airtight container,
or frozen for up to 1 month.

classic oatmeal cookies

makes 10–20 cookies

ingredients
¾ cup butter or margarine, plus extra for greasing
generous 1¹/₃ cup raw brown sugar
1 egg
4 tbsp water
1 tsp vanilla extract
4½ cups rolled oats
1 cup all-purpose flour, sifted
1 tsp salt
½ tsp baking soda

1 Preheat the oven to 350°F/180°C and grease a large baking sheet.

2 Cream the butter and sugar together in a large mixing bowl. Beat in the egg, water, and vanilla extract until the mixture is smooth.

For a sweeter option, drizzle with melted chocolate.

> 3 In a separate bowl, mix the oats, flour, salt, and baking soda. Gradually stir the oat mixture into the creamed mixture until thoroughly combined.

> 4 Place well-spaced tablespoonfuls of the mixture onto the prepared baking sheet. Bake in the preheated oven for 15 minutes, or until golden brown. Remove from the oven and cool on a wire rack.

marzipan whirls

makes 8 whirls

ingredients

generous ½ cup unsalted
  butter, softened
2 tbsp superfine sugar

½ tsp almond extract
scant 1 cup all-purpose flour,
  sifted
1 tbsp milk, to mix

2 tbsp almond paste
4 tsp apricot jam, warmed
confectioners' sugar, sifted,
  for dusting

>1 Preheat the oven to 375°F/190°C. Place 8 paper liners in a shallow muffin pan.

>2 Place the butter, superfine sugar, and almond extract in a food processor and process until pale and fluffy.

>3 Add the flour and process to a soft dough, adding milk if necessary.

>4 Spoon the mixture into a piping bag fitted with a large star vegetable tip.

> **5** Pipe the mixture in a spiral around the sides of each liner, leaving a dip in the center.

> **6** Cut the almond paste into 8 cubes and press one into the center of each whirl.

> **7** Bake in the preheated oven for 15–20 minutes, until pale and golden. Lift the cakes onto a wire rack to cool.

> **8** Once the cakes have cooled, spoon a little of the apricot jam into the center of each.

Dust the cakes with confectioners' sugar and serve.

iced cherry rings

makes 15–18 rings

ingredients
½ cup unsalted butter, plus
  extra for greasing
scant ½ cup superfine sugar

1 egg yolk
finely grated rind of ½ lemon
scant 1½ cups all-purpose flour,
  plus extra for dusting

¼ cup finely chopped
  candied cherries

icing
½ cup confectioners' sugar,
  sifted
1½ tbsp lemon juice

> **1** Preheat the oven to 400°F/200°C. Lightly grease two baking sheets.

> **2** Cream together the butter and superfine sugar until pale and fluffy. Beat in the egg yolk and lemon rind.

> **3** Sift in the flour, stir, then add the candied cherries, mixing with your hands to a soft dough.

> **4** Roll out the dough on a lightly floured surface to about ¼ inch/5 mm thick. Stamp out 3¼-inch/8-cm rounds with a cookie cutter.

>5 Stamp out the center of each round with a 1-inch/2.5-cm cutter and place the rings on the prepared baking sheets. Reroll any trimmings and cut more cookies.

>6 Bake in the preheated oven for 12–15 minutes, until firm and golden brown.

>7 Let cool on the baking sheets for 2 minutes, then transfer to a wire rack to finish cooling.

>8 For the icing, mix the confectioners' sugar to a smooth paste with the lemon juice. Drizzle over the cookies and let stand until set.

Serve with tea or coffee as a
mid-morning treat.

chocolate hazelnut
oatmeal cookies

makes 16–18 cookies

ingredients
6 tbsp unsalted butter, plus
  extra for greasing
$2/3$ cup chocolate hazelnut
  spread
2 cups rolled oats
scant $2/3$ cup chopped,
  blanched hazelnuts

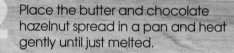

>1 Preheat the oven to 400°F/200°C. Grease a baking sheet.

>2 Place the butter and chocolate hazelnut spread in a pan and heat gently until just melted.

You can store the cookies in an airtight container for up to 2 weeks.

> 3 Add the rolled oats and hazlenuts to the chocolate mixture and stir to combine thoroughly.

> 4 Shape the mixture into 16–18 equal-size balls, then press onto the baking sheet. Bake in the preheated oven for 10–12 minutes, remove from the oven, and let stand until firm before transferring to a wire rack to finish cooling.

cranberry & pine nut biscotti

makes 18–20 biscotti

ingredients

butter or oil, for greasing
scant ½ cup light brown sugar
1 large egg

1 cup all-purpose flour
½ tsp baking powder
1 tsp ground allspice
scant ½ cup dried cranberries

scant ½ cup pine nuts, toasted

>1 Preheat the oven to 350°F/180°C. Grease a baking sheet.

>2 Beat together the sugar and egg until pale and thick enough to form a trail.

>3 Sift the flour, baking powder, and allspice and fold into the mixture.

>4 Stir in the cranberries and pine nuts and mix lightly to a smooth dough.

>5 With lightly floured hands, shape the mixture into a long roll, about 11 inches/ 28 cm long. Press to flatten slightly.

>6 Lift the dough onto the baking sheet and bake in the preheated oven for 20–25 minutes, until golden.

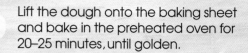

>7 Cool for 3–4 minutes, then cut into ⅝-inch/ 1.5-cm thick slices and arrange on the baking sheet.

>8 Bake in the oven for 10 minutes, or until golden. Remove from the oven, transfer to a wire rack, and let cool.

When cool, store the biscotti in an airtight container for up to 2–3 weeks.

mini florentines

makes 20–30 florentines

ingredients

5½ tbsp butter
1/3 cup superfine sugar
2 tbsp golden raisins or raisins

3 tbsp chopped candied
  cherries
1 oz/ 25 g preserved ginger,
  finely chopped

3 tbsp sunflower seeds
scant 1 cup slivered almonds
2 tbsp heavy cream

6 oz/175 g semisweet dark
or milk chocolate, broken
into pieces

> 1 Preheat the oven to 350°F/180°C. Line two baking sheets.

> 2 Place the butter in a small saucepan and melt over a low heat. Add the sugar, stir until dissolved, then bring to a boil.

> 3 Remove from the heat and stir in the golden raisins, candied cherries, preserved ginger, sunflower seeds, and almonds. Mix well, then beat in the cream.

> 4 Place well-spaced teaspoons of the mixture onto the prepared baking sheets. Bake in the preheated oven for 10–12 minutes, or until light golden brown.

>**5** Remove from the oven and, while still hot, use a circular cookie cutter to pull in the edges to form perfect circles. Let cool and become crisp before removing from the baking trays.

>**6** Put the chocolate in a heatproof bowl set over a saucepan of gently simmering water and stir until melted. Spread most of the chocolate onto a sheet of parchment paper.

>**7** When the chocolate is on the point of setting, place the cookies flat-side down on the chocolate and let it harden completely.

>**8** Cut around the florentines and remove from the parchment paper. Spread the remaining chocolate on the coated side of the florentines, using a fork to mark waves. Let set.

Serve or present as a gift in a pretty box.

chocolate chip cookies

makes 8 cookies

ingredients
unsalted butter, melted,
   for greasing
1¼ cups all-purpose flour, sifted
1 tsp baking powder
½ cup margarine, melted
scant ½ cup light brown sugar
55 g/2 oz caster sugar
½ tsp vanilla extract
1 egg
4½ oz/125 g semisweet dark
   chocolate chips

> **1** Preheat the oven to 375°F/190°C. Line and lightly grease two baking sheets.

> **2** Place all of the ingredients in a large mixing bowl and beat until well combined.

Serve or store in an airtight box.

>3 Place well-spaced tablespoonfuls of the mixture onto the prepared baking sheets.

>4 Bake in the preheated oven for 10–12 minutes, or until golden brown. Transfer to a wire rack and let cool.

breads

>4

>5

>6

crusty white bread

makes 1 loaf

ingredients

1 egg
1 egg yolk
²/₃–1 cup lukewarm water

3½ cups white bread flour,
  sifted, plus extra for dusting
1½ tsp salt
2 tsp sugar
1 tsp active dry yeast

2 tbsp butter, diced
oil, for greasing

>1 Place the egg and egg yolk in a pitcher and beat lightly to mix. Add enough water to make up to 1¼ cups. Stir well.

>2 Place the flour, salt, sugar, and yeast in a large bowl. Add the butter and rub it in with your fingertips until the mixture resembles fine breadcrumbs.

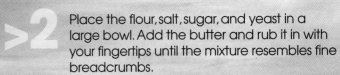

>3 Make a well in the center, add the egg mixture, and work to a smooth dough. Turn out onto a lightly floured surface and knead well for about 10 minutes, until smooth.

>4 Brush a bowl with oil. Shape the dough into a ball, place in the bowl, cover, and let rise in a warm place for 1 hour, or until doubled in volume.

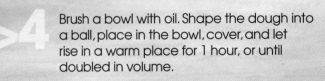

>**5** Preheat the oven to 425°F/220°C. Oil a 9 × 5 × 3-inch/23 × 13 × 8-cm loaf pan. Turn out the dough onto a lightly floured surface and knead for 1 minute, until smooth.

>**6** Shape the dough so it is the same length as the loaf pan and three times the width. Fold the dough in three widthwise and place it in the pan with the join underneath.

>**7** Cover and let stand in a warm place for 30 minutes, until the dough has risen above the pan.

>**8** Place in the preheated oven and bake for 30 minutes, or until firm and golden brown. Transfer to a wire rack and let cool.

Cut into thick slices and serve.

braided poppy seed bread

makes 1 loaf

ingredients

scant 1^2/$_3$ cups white bread
flour, plus extra for dusting
1 tsp salt
2 tbsp skimmed milk powder
1½ tbsp superfine sugar

1 tsp dry active yeast
¾ cup lukewarm water
2 tbsp vegetable oil, plus extra
for greasing
5 tbsp poppy seeds

topping

1 egg yolk
1 tbsp milk
1 tbsp superfine sugar
2 tbsp poppy seeds

>1 Sift the flour and salt together into a bowl and stir in the milk powder, sugar, and yeast. Make a well in the center, pour in the water and oil, and stir until the dough begins to come together.

>2 Add the poppy seeds and knead until fully combined and the dough leaves the side of the bowl. Turn out onto a lightly floured surface and knead for about 10 minutes, until smooth.

>3 Brush a bowl with oil. Shape the dough into a ball, put it in the bowl, cover, and let rise in a warm place for 1 hour, or until doubled in volume.

>4 Oil a baking sheet. Turn out the dough onto a lightly floured surface, punch down, and knead for 1–2 minutes. Divide into 3 equal pieces and shape each into a rope 10–12 inches/25–30 cm long.

>5 Place the ropes side by side and press together at one end. Braid the dough, pinch the other end together, and tuck underneath.

>6 Put the loaf on the prepared baking sheet, cover, and let rise in a warm place for 30 minutes. Meanwhile, preheat the oven to 400°F/200°C.

>7 For the topping, beat the egg yolk with the milk and sugar. Brush the egg glaze over the top of the loaf and sprinkle with the poppy seeds.

>8 Bake in the preheated oven for 30–35 minutes, until golden brown. Transfer to a wire rack and let cool.

Serve plain or toasted as a
lunchtime treat.

pesto & olive soda bread

makes 1 loaf

ingredients
olive oil, for greasing
1¾ cups all-purpose flour
1½ cups whole wheat flour
1 tsp baking soda
½ tsp salt
3 tbsp pesto
1¼ cups buttermilk (approx)
⅓ cup pitted green olives,
  roughly chopped
milk, for glazing

>1 Preheat the oven to 400°F/200°C and line and grease a baking sheet. Sift the flours, baking soda, and salt into a bowl, adding back any bran from the strainer.

>2 Mix the pesto and buttermilk. Stir into the flour with the olives, mixing to a soft dough. Add more liquid if needed.

Serve the soda bread on the day of baking.

>3 Shape the dough into an 8-inch/20-cm round and place on the baking sheet. Flatten slightly and cut a deep cross with a sharp knife.

>4 Brush with milk and bake in the preheated oven for 30–35 minutes, until golden brown. The loaf should sound hollow when tapped underneath.

scallion & parmesan cornbread

serves 16

ingredients

oil, for greasing
1 cup fine cornmeal
1 cup all-purpose flour
4 tsp baking powder

2 tsp celery salt
½ cup grated Parmesan
  cheese
2 eggs, beaten
1¾ cups milk

4 tbsp butter, melted
1 bunch scallions, chopped
ground black pepper

>1 Preheat the oven to 375°F/190°C. Grease a 9-inch/23-cm square baking pan.

>2 Sift the cornmeal, flour, baking powder, celery salt, and pepper into a bowl and stir in 1/3 cup of the Parmesan.

>3 Beat together the eggs, milk, and melted butter.

>4 Add the egg mixture to the dry ingredients and stir well to mix evenly.

>5 Stir in the chopped scallions and spread the mixture evenly into the pan.

>6 Sprinkle the remaining Parmesan over the mixture. Bake in the preheated oven for 30–35 minutes, or until firm and golden.

Cut the cornbread into squares and
serve warm.

rye bread

makes 1 loaf

ingredients

5 cups rye flour
scant 1²/₃ cups white bread
 flour, plus extra for dusting

2 tsp salt
2 tsp soft light brown sugar
1½ tsp active dry yeast
scant 2 cups lukewarm water

2 tsp vegetable oil, plus extra
 for greasing
1 egg white
1 tbsp cold water

>1 Sift the flours and salt together into a bowl. Add the sugar and yeast and stir to mix. Make a well in the center and pour in the water and oil.

>2 Stir until the dough begins to come together, then knead until it leaves the side of the bowl. Turn out onto a lightly floured surface and knead for 10 minutes, until elastic and smooth.

>3 Brush a bowl with oil. Shape the dough into a ball, put it in the bowl, cover, and let rise in a warm place for 2 hours, or until doubled in volume.

>4 Oil a baking sheet. Turn out the dough onto a lightly floured surface and punch down, then knead for 10 minutes.

> **5** Shape the dough into a ball, put it on the prepared baking sheet, and cover. Let rise in a warm place for another 40 minutes, or until doubled in volume.

> **6** Meanwhile, preheat the oven to 375°F/190°C. Beat the egg white with 1 tablespoon of water in a bowl.

> **7** Bake the loaf in the preheated oven for 20 minutes, then remove from the oven and brush the top with the egg white glaze. Return to the oven and bake for another 20 minutes.

> **8** Brush the top of the loaf with the glaze again and return to the oven for another 20–30 minutes, until the crust is a rich brown color. Transfer to a wire rack to cool.

Serve with good quality butter or a topping of your choice.

irish soda bread

makes 1 loaf

ingredients
butter, melted, for greasing
3¼ cups all-purpose flour, plus
  extra for dusting
1 tsp salt
1 tsp baking soda
1¾ cups buttermilk

>1 Preheat the oven to 425°F/220°C. Lightly grease a baking sheet.

>2 Sift the dry ingredients into a mixing bowl. Make a well in the center, pour in most of the buttermilk, and mix well, using your hands. The dough should be very soft but not too wet. If necessary, add the remaining buttermilk.

Serve in slices with butter and a sweet or savory topping.

>3 Turn out the dough onto a floured surface and knead until smooth. Shape into an 8-inch/20-cm round.

>4 Place the bread on the prepared baking sheet, cut a cross in the top, and bake in the preheated oven for 25–30 minutes.

191

pumpkin &
seed twist

makes 1 loaf

ingredients

2¼ cups peeled and diced
  pumpkin
1 tsp fennel seeds

grated rind of 1 lemon
2 tbsp honey
3½ cups strong bread
  flour

½ tsp salt
1 envelope active dry yeast
1¼ cups lukewarm water
  (approx)

oil, for greasing
milk, for glazing
2 tbsp pumpkin and sunflower
  seeds

>1 Steam the pumpkin for 10 minutes, or until tender. Drain thoroughly.

>2 Mash the pumpkin and stir in the fennel seeds, lemon rind, and honey.

>3 Sift the flour and salt into a bowl and stir in the yeast. Add the pumpkin mixture.

>4 Stir in enough water to make a soft dough and knead on a floured surface until smooth.

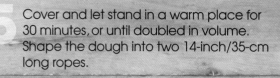 **>5** Cover and let stand in a warm place for 30 minutes, or until doubled in volume. Shape the dough into two 14-inch/35-cm long ropes.

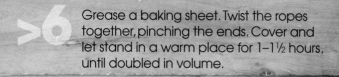 **>6** Grease a baking sheet. Twist the ropes together, pinching the ends. Cover and let stand in a warm place for 1–1½ hours, until doubled in volume.

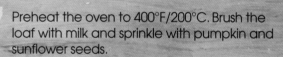 **>7** Preheat the oven to 400°F/200°C. Brush the loaf with milk and sprinkle with pumpkin and sunflower seeds.

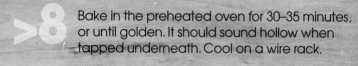 **>8** Bake in the preheated oven for 30–35 minutes, or until golden. It should sound hollow when tapped underneath. Cool on a wire rack.

Serve the loaf sliced with a hearty winter
soup, or for an unusual breakfast.

stromboli with salami, roasted bell peppers & cheese

makes 1 loaf

ingredients
3½ cups white bread flour, sifted
1 envelope active dry yeast
2 tsp sea salt flakes
3 tbsp olive oil, plus extra for brushing
1½ cups lukewarm water

filling
3 oz/85 g thinly sliced Italian salami
6 oz/75 g mozzarella cheese, chopped
1 oz/25 g basil leaves

2 red bell peppers, roasted, peeled, seeded, and sliced (or roasted peppers from a jar)
freshly ground black pepper

> **1** Mix the flour, yeast, and 1½ teaspoons of salt, then stir in the oil with enough water to make a soft dough.

> **2** Knead the dough on a floured surface until smooth. Cover and let stand in a warm place for 1 hour, or until doubled in volume.

> **3** Knead lightly for 2–3 minutes, until smooth. Cover and let stand for another 10 minutes.

> **4** Roll out the dough to a rectangle about 15 x 10 inches/38 x 25 cm in size and ½ inch/1 cm thick.

>5 Preheat the oven to 400°F/200°C. Spread the salami over the dough and top with the mozzarella, basil, and roasted bell peppers. Season with black pepper.

>6 Grease a baking sheet. Roll the dough up firmly from the long side, pinch the ends, and place on a baking sheet with the join underneath. Cover and let stand for 10 minutes.

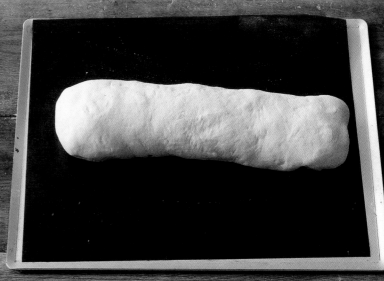

>7 Pierce the roll deeply several times with a skewer.

>8 Brush with oil and sprinkle with the remaining salt. Bake in the preheated oven for 30–35 minutes, or until firm and golden. Cool on a wire rack.

Serve the bread warm and cut
into thick slices.

feta & olive biscuits

makes 8 biscuits

ingredients
butter, for greasing
generous 2¾ cups self-rising
   flour
¼ tsp salt
6 tbsp butter
generous ¼ cup chopped,
   pitted black olives
1½ oz/40 g sun-dried tomatoes
   in oil, drained and chopped
½ cup drained and crumbled
   feta cheese
scant 1 cup milk, plus extra
   for glazing
ground black pepper

> **1** Preheat the oven to 425°F/220°C. Grease a baking sheet.

> **2** Sift the flour, salt, and pepper into a bowl and rub in the butter evenly with your fingers.

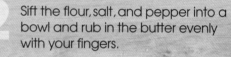

Serve the biscuits fresh and warm, with extra butter if needed.

>3 Stir in the olives, tomatoes, and feta, then stir in just enough milk to make a soft, smooth dough.

>4 Roll out on a floured surface to 1¼-inch/ 3-cm thick rectangle. Cut into 2½-inch/6-cm squares. Place on the baking sheet and brush with milk. Bake for 12–15 minutes, until golden brown.

fresh croissants

makes 6 croissants

ingredients

3½ cups white bread flour
  sifted, plus extra
  for dusting
3 tbsp superfine sugar

1 tsp salt
2 tsp easy-blend dried yeast
1¼ cups lukewarm milk
1¼ cups butter, softened, plus
  extra for greasing

1 egg, lightly beaten with
1 tbsp milk, for glazing

>1 Preheat the oven to 400°F/200°C. Mix the dry ingredients in a large bowl, make a well in the center, and add the milk. Mix to a soft dough, adding more milk if too dry.

>2 Knead on a lightly floured work surface until smooth. Place in a large greased bowl, cover, and let stand in a warm place until doubled in volume.

>3 Meanwhile, place the butter between two sheets of parchment paper and flatten with a rolling pin to form a ¼-inch thick/5-mm rectangle. Set aside in the refrigerator until required.

>4 Knead the dough for 1 minute. Remove the butter from the refrigerator. Roll out the dough on a well-floured work surface to 18 x 6 inches/45 x 15 cm.

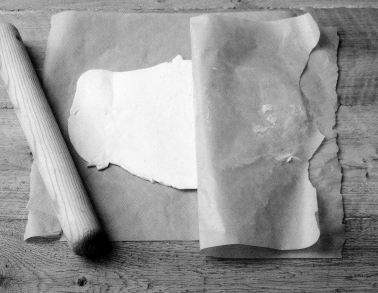

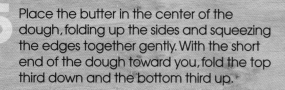

>5 Place the butter in the center of the dough, folding up the sides and squeezing the edges together gently. With the short end of the dough toward you, fold the top third down and the bottom third up.

>6 Give the dough a quarter turn, roll out as big as the original rectangle, and fold again. If the butter feels soft, wrap the dough in plastic wrap and chill. Repeat the rolling process twice more.

>7 Cut the dough in half and roll out each half into a ¼-inch/5-mm thick rectangle. Use a cardboard triangular template, with a base of 4 inches/8 cm and sides of 8 inches/20 cm, to cut out the croissants.

>8 Brush the triangles with the glaze. Roll into croissant shapes, tucking the point underneath. Brush again with the glaze. Place on a baking sheet and let double in volume. Bake in the preheated oven for 15–20 minutes, until golden brown.

Serve with a sweet or savory filling.

cherry & peel spirals

makes 8 spirals

ingredients

4 tbsp melted butter
½ cup chopped candied
  cherries
⅓ cup chopped mixed peel

¼ cup light brown sugar
finely grated rind of 1 lemon
1 tsp ground allspice
1¾ cups bread flour, plus extra
  for flouring

½ tsp salt
1 envelope active dry yeast
½ cup lukewarm milk, plus
  extra for glazing
1 egg, beaten

>**1** Grease an 8-inch/20-cm round cake pan with 1 tbsp butter. Mix together the cherries, peel, sugar, lemon rind, and allspice.

>**2** Sift together the flour and salt, and stir in the yeast. Add the milk, egg, and 2 tablespoons of the butter, and combine.

>**3** Knead on a floured surface until smooth. Cover and let stand in a warm place for 1–1½ hours, or until doubled in volume.

>**4** Knead lightly, then roll out to a 10 x 12-inch/ 25 x 30-cm rectangle.

>5 Brush with the remaining butter and sprinkle with the fruit mixture.

 >6 Roll up from the long side. Cut into 8 slices and arrange in the pan.

>7 Cover and let stand to rise in a warm place until doubled in volume. Preheat the oven to 375°F/190°C.

>8 Brush with milk and bake in the preheated oven for 25–30 minutes, until firm and golden. Cool on a wire rack.

Gently pull the spirals apart
and serve.

cinnamon spiced orange fritters

makes 8 beignets

ingredients
1¾ cups all-purpose flour
1 tsp active dry yeast
1½ tbsp superfine sugar
½ cup lukewarm milk
1 egg, beaten
finely grated rind of 1 small
  orange
1 tsp orange flower water
3 tbsp butter, melted
sunflower oil, for deep-frying
cinnamon sugar, for dusting
orange slices or segments,
  to serve

>**1** Sift the flour into a bowl and stir in the yeast and sugar.

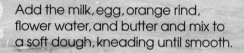

>**2** Add the milk, egg, orange rind, flower water, and butter and mix to a soft dough, kneading until smooth.

Sprinkle with cinnamon sugar and serve hot with orange slices or segments.

>3 Cover and let stand in a warm place until doubled in volume. Roll out on a lightly floured surface to ½ inch/1 cm in thickness, and cut into eight 3-inch/7.5-cm squares.

>4 Heat the oil to 350°F/180°C. Fry the fritters in batches until golden brown. Remove with a slotted spoon and drain on paper towels.

chocolate & saffron brioches

makes 12 brioches

ingredients

pinch of saffron strands
3 tbsp boiling water
4 tbsp butter, melted

1¾ cups bread flour
pinch of salt
1 tbsp superfine sugar
1 envelope active dry yeast

2 eggs, beaten
1 oz/30 g (6 squares) dark
  chocolate
milk, for glazing

>1 Add the saffron to the boiling water and let cool completely.

>2 Lightly brush 12 individual brioche pans or cups in a muffin pan with butter.

>3 Sift the flour, salt, and sugar and stir in the yeast. Add the saffron, saffron liquid, eggs, and remaining butter to make a soft dough.

>4 Knead until smooth, then cover and let stand in a warm place for 1–1½ hours, or until doubled in volume.

>5 Knead briefly then shape three-quarters of the dough into 12 balls. Place in the pans or cups and press a piece of chocolate firmly into each.

>6 Shape the remaining dough into 12 small balls with a pointed end. Brush with milk and press the balls in each brioche, pointed end up, sealing well.

>7 Cover with oiled plastic wrap and let stand in a warm place for 1½ hours, or until doubled in volume.

>8 Preheat the oven to 400°F/200°C. Brush with milk and bake in the preheated oven for 12–15 minutes, until firm and golden.

Turn out the brioches and serve warm—these are a perfect breakfast treat.

crown loaf

serves 9

ingredients
2 tbsp butter, diced, plus extra
  for greasing
scant 1²/₃ cups white bread
  flour
½ tsp salt
1 envelope active dry yeast
½ cup lukewarm milk
1 egg, lightly beaten

filling
4 tbsp butter, softened
¼ cup light brown sugar
2 tbsp chopped hazelnuts
1 tbsp crystallized ginger
generous ⅓ cup chopped
  mixed peel
1 tbsp dark rum or brandy

icing
1 cup confectioners' sugar,
  sifted
1–2 tbsp lemon juice

> **1** Grease a baking sheet. Sift the flour and salt into a bowl. Stir in the yeast. Rub in the diced butter with your fingertips. Add the milk and egg and mix to form a dough.

> **2** Place the dough in a greased bowl, cover, and let stand in a warm place for 40 minutes, or until doubled in volume.

> **3** Punch down lightly for 1 minute. Roll out to a 12 x 9-inch/30 x 23-cm rectangle.

> **4** For the filling, cream the butter and sugar until light and fluffy. Stir in the hazelnuts, ginger, mixed peel, and rum.

> 5 Spread the filling over the dough, leaving a
1-inch/2.5-cm border.

> 6 Roll up the dough, starting from one of the
long edges, into a sausage shape. Cut into
slices at 2-inch/5-cm intervals, and place in a
circle on the prepared baking sheets with the
slices just touching.

> 7 Cover and let stand in a warm place for
30 minutes. Meanwhile, preheat the oven
to 375°F/190°C. Bake the loaf in the
preheated oven for 20–30 minutes, or
until golden.

> 8 For the icing, mix the sugar with enough
lemon juice to form a thin icing. Let the loaf
cool slightly before drizzling with the icing. Let
the icing set before serving.

Cut into 9 slices and serve.

scones

makes 9 biscuits

ingredients

3¼ cups all-purpose flour, plus
  extra for dusting
½ tsp salt
2 tsp baking powder
4 tbsp butter
2 tbsp superfine sugar
generous 1 cup milk, plus extra
  for glazing
strawberry jam and thick
  whipped cream, to serve

>1 Preheat the oven to 425°F/220°C. Sift the flour, salt, and baking powder into a bowl. Rub in the butter using your fingertips until the mixture resembles fine breadcrumbs.

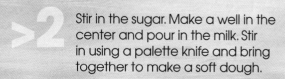

>2 Stir in the sugar. Make a well in the center and pour in the milk. Stir in using a palette knife and bring together to make a soft dough.

Serve freshly baked with strawberry jam and cream as an afternoon treat.

>3 Turn out the dough onto a floured surface and very lightly flatten it until it is ½ inch/1 cm thick. Cut out biscuits using a 2½-inch/6-cm round cutter and place on a lined baking sheet.

>4 Brush with a little milk and bake in the preheated oven for 10–12 minutes, until golden and well risen. Let cool on a wire rack.

Index